THE
MUSIC PARENTS' 𝄞UIDE

A SURVIVAL KIT FOR THE
NEW MUSIC PARENT

THE
MUSIC PARENTS' 𝄞UIDE

A SURVIVAL KIT FOR THE
NEW MUSIC PARENT

ANTHONY MAZZOCCHI

KINMUSIC, LLC
Maplewood, NJ

10 9 8 7 6 5 4 3 2   0 4 0 2 1 5

ISBN: 978-0-9864045-7-3

Printed in the United States of America

Photography by Rob Davidson Photography and Kelly Kroeck Hearn.

♾ This paper meets the requirements of ANSI/NISO Z39.48-1992
(Permanence of Paper)

For Debbie, Luca, and Tahlia

Contents

An Introduction
to "The Guide"

 I have been involved with the teaching of instrumental music for over twenty years. During this time I have witnessed thousands of students start on an instrument each year with the same sparkle in their eyes. I have watched them grow into incredible musicians and also wonderful human beings.

But one short year later, up to 80% of these students are no longer playing.

This massive attrition rate has always startled and perplexed me. Around the fourth, fifth, or sixth grades (in many school districts), up to 100% of students start on an instrument as part of the curriculum. Just about every student opens up their case for the first time and their eyes gleam.

They want to be good at playing their instrument.

But one short year later, up to 60% of these students are no longer playing.

How could this be? Why does this happen?

The answer is not simple, and there are a ton of factors. In my experience, however, there has been one constant: Most parents and students are not armed with enough information to get a solid start on their musical craft.

This is not always the educator's fault.

After all, students may have only one lesson a week of short duration; in groups of varying size. If you live in an area that has music lessons every week in school, your child will probably have a total of sixteen hours of instruction on an instrument for the entire year. **That's a long way from the 10,000 hours it takes for mastery!**

The purpose of this book is to "fill in the gaps" as much as possible with information for parents and students alike during their first year of study. I want to arm all of you with the tools necessary to begin your journey as parents of young musicians.

Understand that my goal is not to create an army of professional musicians—we have plenty of those. Students who stick with a musical instrument through their K–12 experience reap many benefits, including the following:

1. Studies clearly show that musical training develops the part of the brain involved with processing language and can actually wire the brain's circuits in specific and meaningful ways.

2. There is a link between musical training and spatial intelligence (the ability to perceive the world accurately and to form mental pictures of things).

3.   Students of the arts learn to think creatively and to solve problems by imagining various solutions and rejecting outdated rules and assumptions; there is not only one right answer in the arts!

4.   Students who study the arts are more successful on standardized tests such as the SAT; very often they get better grades in school than students who do not study the arts.

5.   Students of music learn how details are put together painstakingly and what constitutes greatness, not mediocrity; through music study, students learn the value of sustained effort to achieve excellence and the concrete rewards of hard work.

6.   Music study enhances teamwork skills and discipline. In order for an ensemble to perform well, all players must work together towards a single goal.

7.   Music provides children with a means of self-expression. Self-esteem is a byproduct of this self-expression.

I want to see more children enjoy a rich life that includes music. The following chapters contain very simple ways to help you understand how to help your child succeed as a young musician. I hope it helps!

The Truth about Musical Talent (FYI: Your Child Has It)

 I am assuming that many of you parents started an instrument at a young age through your school music program.

Did you quit after one or two years? If so, did you quit because you didn't think you were "talented" enough?

Of course you probably remember that one kid who picked up the clarinet or saxophone and was better than everyone in just a few weeks. That kid was so "naturally talented," you thought . . . didn't you?

Well, you were wrong.

Although some people find certain activities easier than others at first, and some people have some physical gifts that others may not have, you are still mistaken about that whole talent thing.

You see, **every child has some degree of musical talent.** Sure, some kids can sing on key really well at a young age or may have a great sense of rhythm right off the bat, but there is more to it than that. At the end of the day, **hard work trumps "natural talent" every single time.** And it takes *time* for students and parents to see that in action. Too many students prematurely abandon the process of getting better, and too many parents let them.

I believe that the reason the majority of students quit an instrument after their first year of playing is not because they do not have musical talent, but rather because:

- their music teacher perhaps is not very good, doesn't have high expectations for their students, doesn't inspire the students enough, or is not thoughtful or systematic in lesson planning for their students;

- the student has no idea how to practice and, therefore, doesn't put in the quality time and becomes frustrated; or

- the students' parents don't have enough knowledge to support their children through the beginning stages of their musical growth.

Some of the greatest musicians, athletes, and businesspeople in the world were (and are) the hardest workers, not necessarily the most naturally gifted people. As a matter of fact, the natural gift that I believe most great people have is that of consistent hard work, patience, and grit. Sure, there are some outliers, but slow, steady, consistent, and dedicated work still had to add up to 10,000 hours (or more) of time on task, and they were on their way to mastering their craft.

But this book is not about helping your child begin a journey to being a professional musician (although if that is what you want, this applies). It's about that moment you hear your child play an instrument for the first time and being prepared for it to sound really, really rough. And it may sound rough for a few weeks, or even a few months, *but that does not mean that your child isn't talented.*

Hey, maybe they will sound pretty good at first—and if that is the case, take out the earplugs and celebrate with them! But at some point, when the music assigned gets a little tough, it *will* be rough and it *will* be time to embrace that wonderful teaching moment where you explain what having "grit" means to your child.

The truth is that your child probably (hopefully) heard an instrument played beautifully before they chose it. The performer probably made it look easy, and your child (and maybe you?) expected that it might sound something like that when they picked it up for the first time—and it didn't. In a world of immediate gratification, this is your moment as a parent to embrace music education as a vehicle to help your child learn every beautiful life skill there is: self-discipline, hard work, compassion, responsibility, and pride, to name a few.

Every day you help your child pick up their instrument and play for a few minutes is a day they come closer to sounding better. Over time, when they *do* sound better, someone may look at your child and mistakenly remark on how naturally talented they must be.

Then you can help set them straight.

Why Students Really Quit Their Musical Instrument (and How Parents Can Prevent It)

 Every year almost 100% of public school students begin an instrument through their school's music program (if a program exists). One or two years later, up to 80% of students quit; unable to enjoy all that music education has to offer for the rest of their K–12 schooling, if not beyond.

During my time as an educator and administrator, parents and students have shared with me several reasons why the child quit their musical instrument, including:

the student is not musically talented (or at least thought
  they weren't);
the student is too busy with other activities;
the student hates practicing (or the parents grow weary
  of begging the child to practice);
the student doesn't like their teacher;
and there's more . . .

But the real reasons that students quit is often beyond their own understanding. In order for a child to be musically successful, it is up to teachers and parents to create memorable experiences that lead students to want to continue on their instrument, especially during the early years of study.

Here are reasons students quit, and ways to combat them:

- **Parents don't see music as a core subject.** The sad truth is that many non-music teachers and administrators do not find music as important as math or English, but parents need to. Besides, you wouldn't let your child quit math, would you? (Though many kids would jump at that opportunity.) Music is a core subject . . . period. The more parents treat it as such, the less students will quit.

- **Students don't know how to get better.** Without the proper tools and practice habits to get better at *anything*, students will become frustrated and want to quit. It is the role of the music educator *and* the parents to give students ownership over their learning. Teachers must teach students *why, how, where, and when* to practice, and parents must obtain minimal knowledge about how students learn music in order to properly support them at home.

- **Parents and students think they aren't musically talented.** Sure, there are some kids who pick up an instrument and sound decent immediately, but they will hit a wall later and have to work hard to overcome it. Most everyone else won't sound that great at first. Playing a musical instrument is a craft that, if practiced correctly, is something that *all* children can find success in. As long as students know how to practice and do so regularly, they will get better.

- **Students discontinue playing over the summer.**
Statistics show that students who do not read over
the summer find themselves extremely behind once
school starts. The same goes for playing an instrument.
A year of musical instruction can quickly go down
the tubes over summer vacation if students do not
find small ways to play once in a while. Picking up
an instrument for the first time after a long layoff
can be so frustrating that a student will not want to
continue into the next school year.

- **The instrument is in disrepair.** A worn down cork,
poorly working reed, or small dent can wreak havoc
on a child's playing ability. Sometimes the malfunction
is so subtle that the student thinks they are doing
something wrong, and frustration mounts. Students,
parents, and teachers need to be aware of the basics
of instrument maintenance and be on top of repairs
when needed.

- **Teachers don't create enough performance opportunities during the year.** The best way to
motivate students musically is through performance.
Weeks or even months on end of practicing without
performing for an audience gets old very quickly,
and student will definitely quit. Teachers should
schedule performances every six weeks or so in order
for students to stay engaged and practicing. Parents
can help by creating small performance opportunities
at home—a Friday night dinner concert or a planned
performance for visiting family members are great
ideas.

- **There is not enough "fun" music to practice.**
It's very important for parents to be aware of music

that interests their child because it exists in sheet music form for download or purchase. It's important that all students play music that aligns with their interests in addition to other pieces that are worked on in school.

- **Other activities are pulling at the child.** Between art lessons, sports, karate, and other activities, parents grow weary of having "one more thing" to be on top of schedule-wise. Parents need to understand that the enduring social and psychological benefits of music are as enormous as those of sports. Budget time accordingly, and children will have at least ten minutes a day to practice an instrument, for sure.

Much like any worthwhile venture, practicing a musical instrument has its ups and downs. Kids need to be reminded to practice, of course, but they should not be constantly pushed, and they should not be completely left alone. It's a balancing act where sometimes the parents will need to give their child a break for a few days and other times will need to bribe them to practice. Either way, all children are capable of thriving with a musical education, and students will indeed thank their parents for not letting them quit.

How to Choose Which Musical Instrument to Play

Even though this was mentioned in a previous chapter, it bears repeating:

Everyone is capable of playing an instrument at a proficient level with the right support and mindful practice.

Therefore, the first step is the most crucial: picking an instrument that suits your child's identity and personality, and picking one that they want to play (hopefully for a long time!).

While that sounds like serious business, also remember that students change instruments all the time; this is not exactly do-or-die here . . . yet. Anyone is allowed to change their mind (just not too much).

Students Must Actively Be Involved in the Process

Many schools deal with the instrument-choice issue differently. When the decision is made to start an instrument, the most important thing is to have the student be involved in the process. The second most important thing is to be aware of the many instruments available.

Not only should a parent and student learn about the different instruments prior to making a decision, but the child should handle and play several instruments.

It is crucial that your child start by playing an instrument that they are excited about learning. Many students already think they know what type of instrument they want to play, but their decision may not be as educated as you might think. After all, if you ask most younger kids what instrument they want to play, they will usually say "sax" or "drums"! Those instruments are more prominently featured in our culture in general. Your child may not even know what an oboe or a French horn is yet!

Some of the more not-so-ideal situations occur when one teacher demonstrates all of the instruments to the students. Because the teacher probably specializes in only one instrument (maybe two), the likelihood of students hearing an instrument played at its best is very small.

No one can make an educated decision about the instrument that they want to study without hearing it played beautifully!

Students need to hear instruments played to their absolute, full potential, both before choosing it and also during their weekly study. This can happen in one of a few ways:

- going to a live concert;

- attending an instrument "petting zoo" hosted by a local music store, where students can try out each instrument and hear them played by professionals (if your local store doesn't do this yet, ask them to . . . They will probably think it's a great idea!);

- signing on to YouTube to check out performances (there is a lot of garbage on there, too. Make sure you surf around a bit); or

- going to a local college to watch a band/orchestra performance.

The Size of the Child/Instrument Matters

One of the biggest reasons students quit playing their instruments is unnecessary frustration. Instruments are challenging enough to begin with, so any physical limitations that could be avoided should be considered ahead of time. Consider these points:

- A youngster who lacks fine motor coordination may struggle with a violin but manage an alto saxophone more easily. But a tenor sax or baritone sax for a smaller person may be too much, too soon. The young saxophonist is advised to begin with the alto instrument before moving to the larger instruments.

- The weight and finger or arm stretch of tuba, trombone, and bassoon can be daunting and uncomfortable for those with smaller physiques.

- A student's clarinet may squeak a lot if their fingers are extremely skinny and cannot cover the holes well enough. Without knowing this in advance, they may get frustrated and quit. The student would manage much better with the covered holes found on flutes and saxophones.

Playing an incompatible instrument can cause tension, leading to fatigue, frustration, and quitting. Tests are available through some music shops and schools to assess a student's suitability to the instrument of choice. I strongly advise parents to look into this to the best of their ability before paying money for an instrument.

Sax and Drums

There is nothing at all wrong with children wanting to play sax or drums, but please remember this:

- If they start on flute or clarinet, there is a good chance that sax will seem easy in comparison later . . . then they will be able to play two instruments!

- Drums, when they begin, does not mean drum SET . . . it is usually only a snare and bass drum (especially in a school setting). Make sure you watch some videos of percussionists in bands and orchestras and point this out. It is very different than playing a drum set in a rock band! Percussion instruction includes playing mallet instruments (xylophone, marimba), so make sure there might be an interest there as well.

The most important factor in choosing an instrument is that the student WANTS to learn how to play it and is excited about doing so.

All said and done, if a student really loves a particular instrument's sound, you need to go with that. The other incompatibilities can be overcome with mindful practice.

Should I Rent or Buy Our First Musical Instrument?

 An important decision that parents have to make is whether they should rent or buy an instrument for their child who is just beginning to play.

Renting vs. buying an instrument is an important decision that can impact not only on your finances, but also whether your child stays with (and enjoys) their instrument for years or quits in frustration after a few months.

Naturally, the fear of a child losing interest in the first year or two drives many parents to choose to rent rather than to buy. However, renting for the short term does not always work, and can cost way too much over the long term.

Renting an Instrument

Most students in the US start instrumental music in the fourth, fifth, or sixth grade. Elementary and middle schools frequently have "band rental night" or pass out flyers near the beginning or end of each school year. This is often presented in association with local music stores that rent instruments.

For some parents, the rental option offers a quick and easy way of letting their child get started playing the instrument they have chosen. There is nothing wrong with this, of course, as long as the instruments are of good quality and affordable. Renting in this manner, however, may not be the most cost effective way of getting started.

The typical method for renting a band instrument is a rent-to-own contract. The parent pays a monthly rental fee to the music store or a flat yearly rate. What many parents may not realize about a rent-to-own contract is that by the time they own the instrument (years after starting to rent), they have paid much more in rental fees than it would have cost to buy a brand-new instrument up front. This is because they are paying the full retail price for the instrument instead of the normal selling price. The normal selling price of a band instrument is usually 20–40% *less* than full retail.

In addition, the rental contract usually includes interest charges and insurance fees, even if these are not explicitly spelled out. Parents could pay up to three times as much for an instrument on a rent-to-own plan than if they had just bought a new instrument outright in the first place. If a student stays with an instrument for two years, the rent-to-own option is probably not a good one.

The finish on previously rented instruments may be worn, and more serious repair issues may be present.

Advantages to Renting:

- The convenience factor cannot be beat (you can return the instrument at any time).

- Repairs are usually covered under the rental agreement.

- If the student decides to stop playing before the end of the first year, renting can sometimes be a better financial decision than buying a new instrument.

Buying an Instrument

A major advantage to buying a new instrument is that it gives both students and parents a greater sense of commitment to playing and studying the instrument. This often translates into the student being further encouraged to keep playing the instrument they have chosen. Parents tend to encourage daily practice a bit more, which is a key to long-term engagement in music.

You can buy a new instrument from a music store, a private dealer or the Internet. If you are fortunate enough to have a local music store that carries new instruments, this is a great opportunity to select the instrument of your choice. If possible, ask your child's teacher for advice on brands, or even to accompany you to the store and help in the selection of the best instrument for your child.

Buying online is always a viable alternative. Again, ask your child's teacher for advice on the best student-model instrument. Buy from an online retailer that will allow at least thirty-day returns.

A great alternative to buying a new instrument is to buy a good used instrument. This can be an excellent, cost-effective alternative to buying new. However, if you elect to buy a used instrument, it's important to have your child's music teacher inspect the instrument. It's very frustrating for a beginning student to try to learn on an instrument that leaks, sticks, or has some other mechanical problem.

Advantages to Buying:

- Your child possibly has more motivation to play and take care of the instrument.

- Instruments have good resale value, so you may save a lot of money over renting.

- If your child sticks with the instrument for over two years, you save money over renting.

A final note: **Do not buy a cheap instrument at a non-music retail store!** A fifty dollar instrument is a toy, not a musical instrument. Also, beware of music stores charging full retail for instruments! Do not be scared of buying a better quality instrument used. If it is a good instrument, it was probably taken care of and will play great!

What Do I Do When My Child Brings Their Instrument Home for the First Time?

 What an exciting day! The first day a child receives their instrument is always wonderful. When your child opens that instrument case for the first time, ***they want to be good at playing it.***

It goes without saying that your child will probably want to immediately start playing their instrument. Many times, they have not received their first lesson yet and don't know how to properly handle the instrument. Beware! This is the most common scenario that leads to an instrument breaking. Some of the disrepair may not be evident at first, but it could cause sound quality issues. This leads to frustration on the part of the student, and next thing you know, they are not as excited to play as they once were. We want to do everything in our power as teachers and parents to make sure they maintain that "sparkle in their eyes" about playing an instrument, so properly handling the instrument is of paramount importance.

Many teachers do not spend enough time teaching cleaning, maintaining, and putting together an instrument, so you should reinforce these things with your child. Here are your first steps to learning this process in order to ensure years of playing enjoyment:

- Check out The Music Parents' Guide YouTube channel for videos on handling the instrument.

- Learn how to set the case down properly. (Yes, there is a right and wrong way!)

- Carefully learn how to put the instrument together with your child! It does not take that long. Each instrument has its own "rules." (Clarinets and flutes: don't touch the keys! Trombones: slide care is key.)

- Putting the instrument away poses its own problems as well, so learn how to do this.

There are good and bad ways to even set an instrument down, even if you have learned how to put it together the right way! You may even want to purchase an instrument stand. These stands allow the instrument to be placed the right way and be extremely accessible at all times!

As soon as the slightest thing seems in disrepair, bring the instrument to your teacher or the local music shop.

You should expect to spend a little money every year on lubricants and instrument maintenance. Maintaining the instrument and cleaning it out should be a habit, and can also be fun! I believe that the number one reason students quit at a young age is because their instrument is not working properly, therefore making it too difficult to play.

Enjoy the process of good instrument maintenance and treat your instrument like gold!

What to Expect from Your School Music Teacher

Even if we are not math, English/language arts, or history majors, we as parents have certain expectations about what our children learn about these subjects in school. Dinner-table conversations may include questions about what the teacher taught or how they taught it. Parents have opinions on how or why a subject is taught, and many times will follow up with teachers in order to be able to assist their child at home with these subjects.

When it comes time for music class, however, many parents simply don't know what to expect. Their child will come home with a method book and a piece of music and start playing, and perhaps once in a while the parent will yell from the kitchen, "That didn't quite sound like Hot Cross Buns!"

There are a few things that *all parents* should expect from music teachers in order to assist their child in practicing and to develop healthy dialogue with the music instructor when their child is having a tough time.

How to Put Together and Care for Their Instrument

Without a proper working instrument, students will become frustrated and quit immediately. The first things a teacher should teach a music student is:

- how to open the instrument case correctly;

- how to put their instrument together safely and take it apart; and

- how to clean their instrument daily, weekly, and monthly.

When to Practice

Many teachers use "practice logs" that get sent home in order to ensure students have spent time on their instrument each night. Parents sign off on it and turn it in each week to the teacher. Sometimes these are useful, oftentimes not. This is because mindful practice trumps mindless playing every single time. Meaningful practice is not measured in minutes, but in the number of high quality repetitions a student executes. Parents should expect that teachers have taught students that:

- Five minutes of practice a day is better than one hour once a week.

- Students should embrace routine; they should practice at the same time every day.

- Students learn about having "grit" when they practice at times they want to the least.

What to Practice

What should students be practicing each night? If your child starts out by putting their instrument together and playing a song, they either have not listened to their teacher or the teacher is not teaching students what to practice.

The following are things that **every student must be told to practice daily:**

- scales;

- fundamental exercises suited to their instrument (lip slurs for brass players, fundamental bowing exercises for strings, etc.);

- an exercise from a method book;

- sections of pieces of music to be performed at the concert; and

- fun stuff that the student likes (play-along songs, improvisation, etc.).

The list above, in that order, is a perfect practice session of at least fifteen minutes. Parents should expect that their child is learning this at school.

How to Practice

Any school teacher worth their salt will teach students *how* to practice (it is this author's opinion that not enough do). This includes:

- how to use a metronome;

- how to use a tuner;

- how to set goals for each practice session (what should the student be able to accomplish at the end of their session that they could not accomplish before?);

- how to break sections down into little "chunks," then put it back into the larger piece; and

- how to practice bits at a very slow tempo, then increase the tempo systematically (parents, if you recognize the piece right off the bat, it is possible that they are practicing it too fast).

Teachers should also discuss with students how the brain works; repetition is key. Students have to practice sections of music for days in a row until the skill is engraved in the brain.

What to Listen to

Teachers should point students toward great musicians who play the instrument that the student is studying. Through the internet, young people now have access to audio and video of the great performers at their fingertips. Students should spend five to ten minutes every day listening to or watching great performers. This is a fantastic family bonding time where even the parents will hear beautiful music they never knew existed!

The few items listed above can give parents a little more "ammo," allowing them to adequately check student progress as well as the quality of teaching their child is receiving. This leads to successful music students who continue to play for quite a long time. It also crosses over to other subjects; routine, repetition, and grit are behaviors we want all of our children to learn, and most of the time they are taught these through music!

Public and private school music teachers have many demands put upon them, from writing lesson plans to meeting deadlines for administrators. That said, they are also interested in creating great young musicians and ensembles. Just as academic teachers should not be "teaching to the test," music teachers should not "teach to the concert." With correct attention to the fundamentals of playing the instrument, the concert becomes easy!

Keep your ears out for how your child is practicing!

Why Parents Shouldn't Fear the Pull-Out Music Lesson in School

The pull-out lesson is one of the only ways that public and private schools can start students on an instrument. The band or strings teacher will set up a schedule so four to five students at a time can receive a half hour lesson once a week. Most of the time, this is the child's first-ever music lesson, where they learn how to put the instrument together, make a sound, learn to note read, learn *études*, etc.. As the child moves to middle school, the pull-out lesson is used to work on securing a good fundamental approach to the instrument beyond the full band or orchestra class.

When students begin taking music lessons in school, parents, teachers, and even administrators may become worried that the student will fall behind academically if they attend the pull-out lesson.

On the surface, this may seem like a rational concern, but you don't need to worry! **There is no data that shows that students suffer academically from half hour a week of pull-out lessons.**

If scheduled correctly, students are pulled out of class for music lessons once a week on a rotating basis. This means that a student may miss period one during the first week, period two the second week, period three the next week, and so on. Therefore, any one student will miss a half hour of one subject once a month when the lesson schedule is executed the right way.

Let's think about that for a second. This means:

- A student being pulled out for music misses *less* class time than an entire class going on a field trip or attending an assembly.

- When a teacher is absent for a six-hour school day, that is the equivalent of a student being pulled out *twelve times* for music lessons.

- If a student attends every single pull-out lesson in a school year, they will have somewhere between twelve to fourteen hours of instruction on their instrument (that is not much time at all).

It is important for parents to let their child know that when students are dismissed for instrumental music, they are not leaving instruction, but rather moving to a different classroom in another area of the building. Music, after all, is as much of a class as anything else!

What Does a Great Education Mean to You?

We always hear buzzwords like "critical thinking skills" and "inquisitive, lifelong learning," and that is exactly what a musical education provides. Taking a half hour once a week to study music, as opposed to memorizing facts for the next test, is a healthy thing.

There is no way to truly quantify what learning an instrument does to your child's brain (although a lot of progress is being made in this regard), therefore public school administrators have a difficult time fitting it into the grand scheme of their test-prep world. Your child's brain development should not suffer as a consequence!

At the end of the day, memorizing facts and mastering test-taking skills is rarely an indicator of future success. Again, a half hour a week of a different approach to learning is an extremely important half hour spent for your child.

What to Expect from Teachers

Most of the time, the music teacher will work with other teachers when a student is falling behind in their work in other classes (which is rarely the case). They should also work with parents when a student is doing poorly in classroom subjects by changing the lesson time or recommending an outside tutor to help with the class(es) the child is having trouble in. Most great music educators are an active part of the school community, so principals and fellow teachers are often more willing to negotiate student time if they believe the music instructor is truly interested in students' welfare.

The benefits of music instruction are so varied and wonderful. Parents should absolutely give their children a chance at the instrumental pull-out lessons and see how it goes. The lessons provide a great variance to the school day only one time per week. When you go see and hear your child's first school concert, you will see how worth it the lessons were!

How to Give Ownership of Practicing an Instrument to Your Child

 Practicing a musical instrument regularly is tough for most kids. That *does not* mean that when your child is giving you a hard time about practicing it means that they hate music and want to quit. They just don't like practicing, and that's okay . . . for now.

There are many ways to get your child to practice. You can force them, create a sticker chart, or even bribe them (yes, this works—don't feel guilty if you do it). Some days will be easier than others, and sometimes you will have to lose the battle in order to win the war. But eventually, your goal should be to give your child ownership of their own learning.

What Is "Ownership of Learning"?

Basically, when a student understands "why," "how," "where," and "when" to practice, they have been given power. They will feel a sense of responsibility, which will then lead to self-motivation and routine. Ideally we want our children to have ownership over their own learning in every aspect of life, and music education is a wonderful way to teach this!

Why Practice?

Let's use a sports analogy. Basketball players must consistently work out in the weight room, run miles a day, and shoot hundreds of free throws a week in order to be physically and mentally ready for each game. Musicians use small muscles (embouchure, fingers, etc.) that need a constant regular workout as well. Especially at young ages, musicians' muscles develop very quickly with regular practice, so improvement is very obvious. Students need to practice so they are ready for the game (performance). The more performances (which can include Friday night dinner concerts at home), the more likely your child will understand the need for practice, so keep that in mind!

When to Practice?

Ideally, practice should happen every day. In our house, we are happy with five days a week for our young children. Sometimes we make it to seven, but if it's late and our kids (or the parents!) are tired and cranky, we have a two-day buffer. That works for some and not others, but everyday practice may not happen for beginners or older students who have decided that music is a hobby. The bottom line is that we as parents need to help our children get in the habit of practicing, just like they brush their teeth and do their other homework.

Practice should occur at the same time every day, if possible. Making practice part of the child's daily routine is key. Getting started is always the toughest part of practicing; I always thought that taking the instrument out of the case was the toughest part— once it came out and I started playing, I was set. Purchasing an instrument stand is a great idea. That way the instrument is always out and ready to be played!

How Long Should My Child Practice?

I am a big fan of the "ten-minute rule." Ten minutes of practice a day (for beginners) is better than nothing, and 99% of the time ten minutes turns into twenty minutes! As long as your teacher gives clear assignments, ten minutes will certainly extend to a half an hour easily.

Many school music teachers send home practice charts that have to be filled out and returned each week. Awards may be given out for more time on task, or total time practiced each month. Pedagogically speaking, I believe this emphasizes quantity over quality, but it does work for many students.

If you are the type of parent who needs concrete numbers, try this:

- Beginning students = ten minutes a day*

- Middle school students = half hour a day*

- High school students = forty-five minutes to one hour a day*

*If your child shows passion at a young age, or they are getting pretty serious by middle school, these numbers should as much as *triple*.

If the practice is goal related (the child knows they need to learn X scale, X *étude*, and X measures of a band piece), the time will take care of itself. Sitting down to practice with specific goals is *crucial* to successful growth.

Where to Practice?

Ideally, parents should carve out a relatively quiet area with a chair and a sturdy music stand. There should be proper lighting and a place to store extra strings, rosin, music, pencils, markers, notebooks, and a metronome. There should be minimal distractions such as TV, radio, other children, pets, or telephones.

How to Practice

The sooner a child learns *how* to practice, the better! The best tip I can give to parents is this:

Muscle memory and tempo are mutually exclusive. That means everything must be practiced VERY SLOWLY in order for the skill to be successfully "programmed" into the body.

This is very difficult for young children, especially when they are learning to play a song that they recognize.

If mistakes are happening, it is more than likely that the piece is being practiced at a tempo that is too fast.

Students shouldn't always start at the beginning of a piece each time they sit down to practice it. Work should be done on small "snippets" that give them trouble; practicing them slowly, then speeding them up. Hard sections should be broken down into small bits, perhaps even to the point where they are playing single notes. These sections should be repeated many times until the music becomes easy to play. Then the student should put the piece back together and gradually bring it up to tempo.

Sometimes practice happens without making sounds. Students should take time to figure out the fingering of passages note by note. Any time a mistake occurs, your child should feel free to make a note in the music with pencil.

Practice with a metronome is *huge* and leads to tons of improvement! Students should set it at a slow count at first, then gradually increase the pulse until they arrive at the final tempo.

Students should make good use of pencil and markers to indicate places where they keep making the same mistake.

A digital recorder or phone is a great tool to use when practicing. Students can record themselves playing so they can hear problems, particularly regarding to rhythm and notes. This is a lot of fun for them to do, so encourage it!

Students should end practice sessions by playing beautifully a piece of their choice.

Practice Games

Making any chore a game makes it more desirable.

A lot of fun can be had with just three pennies!

First, the student puts three pennies on the left side of the music stand. While practicing a troublesome measure, for every time they play it correctly, they move one penny to the right side of the stand. If they play it again and get it right, they put the next penny on the right side of the stand. If they play it and miss a note or rhythm, then all the pennies go back to the left side. The student must play the measure correctly three times in a row in order to keep the pennies. The next step is to connect the troublesome measure to the measure before it and continue playing.

By the fifth or sixth grade, your child should begin taking ownership over their learning. They need to understand that what you put in is what you get out. It is the parent's job to get their child to that point by ensuring that practice happens daily. Kids won't always understand this at a young age, but parents are doing them such a huge favor by not allowing them to quit. At the very least, children will grow up knowing what it takes to truly achieve something and how to motivate themselves to do things that they might not always want to do.

That is the gift of ownership.

How to Keep Your Child Musically Engaged over the Summer

More than likely, your child will be part of a musical ensemble in school where they will be introduced to the concepts of teamwork, discipline, self-confidence, determination and camaraderie. The more performances a child has, the more they will be motivated to practice in order to contribute their best work to the ensemble.

One of the reasons children discontinue their musical instrument study from one school year to the next is that they take the entire summer off of playing. This leads them to be incredibly "out of shape"—younger players often forget how to play completely and feel as if they are "starting from scratch" by the end of the summer. This can be very frustrating, and may lead your child to want to quit.

Therefore, providing opportunities for your child to continue playing their instrument over the summer is very important. Although regular weekly practice is preferable, you don't need to stress out if they only play for a few weeks or so. As discussed in previous chapters, a small amount of time spent regularly on the instrument is much better than nothing!

Group and ensemble playing over the summer is a fantastic musical *and* social outlet. Lifelong friends are made during many summer activities, and music is certainly no exception.

It's important to ask your music teacher about local playing opportunities, but here are some ideas to help you encourage your child to play their instrument over the summer:

- Many public schools have inexpensive (or free) summer camps with musical ensembles and lessons. You can rarely go wrong with this option.

- There are many community music programs as well. Google "summer music programs" near you; it is preferable if the program includes private lessons.

- Once your child has been playing for a year or two, there are fantastic regional day or sleep-away music camps at all different levels of rigor. My camp, Kinhaven Music School, is for advanced middle and high school musicians, but there are many other varieties out there.

- This may be a great time to arrange for private lessons or find a music mentor for your child. Just a few private lessons will help keep your child interested and playing through the summer.

- Invite your child's friends over to play some music together. The music can be out of their school music books or downloaded from online. It makes for a very cool playdate.

- Have your child give you a lesson on their instrument—the best way for anyone to learn and understand something is to teach it.

- Search for songbooks (preferably with CD accompaniment) that your child likes at your local music store. These accompanied songs can be very fun to play once in a while.

There are a lot of growing music technology companies and app developers out there these days. Using technology is right up your child's alley, so investigate some cool software. For example, SmartMusic is an exciting, interactive software program that many school music programs are using, but it is also great for home use. SmartMusic provides great value for students at all levels. For instance:

- Students practice with background accompaniment and get visual and audio feedback on each piece, which makes practice more meaningful and productive.

- SmartMusic motivates students to continue practicing to improve their scores, similar to a video game, which makes practice more fun.

- Students can practice solos and full band/orchestra pieces while hearing the entire ensemble as they play—it's like performing with a piano or in an actual ensemble!

Listening to music is an important way to continue to fill the brain with beautiful sounds, which is so important in the process of learning to play an instrument. Don't forget to attend some concerts—many are free and outdoors, which makes for a great family outing!

Continuing to play a musical instrument over the summer is potentially the difference between quitting and continuing with the instrument. This additional time away from school with the instrument helps to build upon all the good work that was done during the year and continues to emphasize the concept of routine and self-discipline. It would be a shame to lose all the skills that were built during the year, and just a few days a week of playing over the summer will ensure that your child enjoys another school year with music in his or her life!

There is So Much More . . .

This book is meant to serve as an entry-level primer for parents who are searching for a few guidelines to help their children succeed in their school music program. Of course there is so much more to write and discuss when it comes time to help students become extremely proficient at their instruments, but I believe I have provided enough information here to ensure that every family has a chance to be musically successful.

To supplement this book, I have created a kit of sorts that I hope you will take advantage of. This includes:

- The Music Parents' Guide YouTube Channel—Visit here, early and often, to watch videos that offer tips on putting together and maintaining your instrument, practice advice, beautiful performances, and more!

- The Music Parents' Guide Blog—Educators and musicians from around the nation contribute valuable information here in order to guide parents down their child's musical path. You will find posts about how to search for a private instructor, how to audition

for honors ensembles, what to expect when it comes
to applying for college, and much more.

Finally, you can always feel free to email me with any questions,
comments, concerns, or advice at:

thempguide@gmail.com

Enjoy being a music parent. The gift you are giving your child
is beyond words—that's why it is expressed in music.

About the Author

A **GRAMMY®** nominated music educator, **Anthony Mazzocchi** has performed as a trombonist with the Los Angeles Philharmonic, the New Jersey Symphony, the San Diego Symphony, the San Diego Opera, the Riverside Symphony, and the Key West Symphony. He has also been featured in various Broadway shows, numerous recordings, and several movie soundtracks. Tony has served as faculty or as a frequent guest lecturer at the Juilliard School, the Manhattan School of Music, New York University, and Mannes College of Music. He has taught grades four through into college and has served as a school district administrator of fine and performing arts. Tony has been a consultant for arts organizations throughout the NY/NJ area. He is currently associate director of the John J. Cali School of Music at Montclair State University in New Jersey and co-executive director of the Kinhaven Summer Music School in Weston, Vermont, with his wife, Deborah.